THE NEGRO'S FRIEND

SKETCHES OR THE HISTORY

of

JAMAICA

PART I

SELECTED FROM VARIOUS AUTHORS

GIFT *Certificate*

TO:

_____

_____

_____

FROM:

_____

_____

DATE: _____

Would you like to buy a copy of
**THE NEGRO'S FRIEND; SKETCHES OR
THE HISTORY OF JAMAICA?**

PLEASE VIST:
http://www.diamondbooks.ca

THE NEGRO'S FRIEND

SKETCHES OR THE HISTORY

of

JAMAICA

GIVEN BY:
Wendell Phillips

Wendell Phillips was an American abolitionist, advocate for Native Americans, orator, and attorney. According to George Lewis Ruffin, a Black attorney, Phillips was seen by many Blacks as "the one white American wholly color-blind and free from race prejudice".

SELECTED FROM VARIOUS AUTHORS

DIAMOND BOOKS™

www.diamondbooks.ca

TORONTO, CANADA – 2022

DIAMOND **BOOKS** - CANADA

DIAMOND[TM]
BOOKS

Toronto, ON, CANADA

http://www.**diamondbooks**.ca

BIBLIOGRAPHIC INFORMATION

**THE NEGRO'S FRIEND; SKETCHES OR
THE HISTORY OF JAMAICA**
FIRST PUBLISHED IN 1882.
S. BAGSTER, JUN., PRINTER,
14, BARTHOLOMEW CLOSE. LONDON

PUBLISHED IN CANADA

Published in Canada by DIAMOND BOOKS ™, an imprint

of

DIAMOND PUBLISHERS CANADA

http://www.diamondpublishers.com

DIAMOND BOOKS ™ - REGISTERED TRADEMARK IN CANADA AND WORLDWIDE.

REPUBLISHED EDITION : APRIL, 2022.

PAPERBACK EDITION : ISBN: 978-1-988942-89-6

PRINTED IN CANADA

A COLLECTED COPY OF THIS LITERATURE WAS GIVEN
TO 'BOSTON PUBLIC LIBRARY'
BY
MR. WENDELL PHILLIPS, ON JULY 22, 1882.

SOLD AT THE DEPOSITORY
IN LONDON, ENGLAND.

BY

HARVEY & DARTON,
55, Gracechurch Street;

HOULSTON & SON,
Paternoster-Row;

EDMUND FRY, *Houndsditch;*

E. ALBRIGHT, *Newington-Causeway,
London, and other Booksellers.*

— *Price 1 ½ d. or* 10s. *per* 100.

"Shall not all these take up a parable against him, and a taunting proverb against him, and say, Woe to him that increaseth that which is not his! ... Because thou hast spoiled many nations, all the remnant of the people shall as thee ; because of men's blood, and for the violence of the land, of the city, and of all that dwell therein. ..Woe to him that worketh an evil covetousness to his house. Woe to him that buildeth a town with blood, and stablisheth a city by iniquity!" — Habakkuk ii. 6, 8, 9, 12.

PART I.

CHRISTOPHER COLUMBUS discovered Jamaica in 1494, but made no settlement there.

In 1509, Don Diego Columbus, the son of this extraordinary man, sent seventy Spaniards from St. Domingo to Jamaica, under the command of John d'Esquimel; others soon followed. It seemed as if they all went over to this peaceable island, for no other purpose than to shed human blood. Those barbarians never sheathed their sword while there was one inhabitant left to preserve the memory of a numerous, mild, plain, and hospitable people. In a few years they murdered no less than 60,000 of the original inhabitants.

The Savannahs, which have since been so unproductive and useless; were then the richest spots in the island, and yielded all manner of necessaries, and maintained numerous herds of cattle. It is said that when the English took the island, they killed 20,000 horned cattle in the first four months.

The Spaniards began to purchase Negroes soon after they were settled there.

An early writer on Jamaica, speaking of the climate, says: "Our political arithmeticians imagine, once in seven years there is a revolution of lives in this island; that as many die in that space of time as at once inhabit it; and no doubt the multitude that dies would soon leave the place a desert, did not daily recruits come over from Great Britain. Scarcely a ship arrives, but has passengers who design to settle, and servants for gale, This is a constant supply, and a necessary one; for notwithstanding their vast numbers, the island but slowly settles."

The whole population of the colony did not exceed 1500 persons, with about as many Negroes, in 1655, when the English, under the command of Admiral Penn and General Venables, took the island, and left Colonel Doyley, Governor, who was for some time engaged in completely subduing the Spaniards. In this he was assisted by many of the slaves belonging to the Spaniards; and they being sure of an immediate and cruel death, should they again fall into the hands of their old masters, did all they could against them.

Col. Doyley rewarded some of these, and declared others free; particularly one who greatly assisted him. This man had been slave to one of the most considerable of the Spaniards, and was very much attached to a young female Negro, who had borne him several children, and with whom he lived in as much happiness as the state of slavery affords; when his old master barbarously and wickedly tore the object of his affections from him, and compelled her to live with himself. The husband expressed his indignation in strong terms, but he met with nothing in return but severe whippings; to which he submitted, but sought revenge. During the disturbances occasioned by the English invasion, he got an interview with his once adored wife, and induced her to go to some distance; when, after having told her how sincerely he still loved her, and that he could not bear to see her another's, when she could not be his, he plunged a poniard to her heart, and saw her breathe her last. He then fled to the English, and did them great service in all their engagements, particularly in one, where the sight of his former tyrant having inflamed his revenge,

he flew to the place where he fought, and'
soon laid the vile adulterer at his feet. Col.
Doyley took particular notice of him, made
him free, and gave him a small piece of
ground, upon which he ever afterwards
lived in quiet, but with a thoughtfulness
and melancholy that he could not conquer.

When the Spaniards were compelled to
cede Jamaica to the English, they left there
a number of Negroes and Mulattoes, who
retired into the mountains to preserve their
liberty. Having entered into some
agreements to preserve their union, they.
planted maize and cocoa, in the most
inaccessible parts of their retreats; but
being in want of subsistence till harvest,
they came down into the plain to pillage for
food. The English bore this plunder
impatiently, for they had nothing to spare;
and they declared war against them. Many

were massacred; some submitted; and a few fled back to the rocks. They were soon joined by numbers of slaves, grown desperate by the hardships they endured, or by the dread of punishment. They frequently annoyed the planters by their depredations, and were often pursued, and when taken, or overcome, treated with great cruelty. In this situation was the colony when Trelawney was appointed Governor. This prudent and humane commander was sensible, that men who for near a century had exposed themselves to continual hardships, would never be subdued by open force. He therefore had recourse to conciliating measures. He offered them not only lands as their own property, but likewise liberty and independence. The descendants of these people have been called Maroons. Is it not natural here to observe how strongly the love of liberty prevails in the hearts of men, notwithstanding the most wretched circumstances? These runaways endured more for near the space of a century, than can be found on record of any state or people. They struggled with a superior force, went naked, exposed to the in clemencies of the air, fed on roots and fruits, and cheerfully ventured their lives to secure themselves free.

In the year 1760, the Negro slaves, exasperated at the ill usage they met with from the English, resolved to be free likewise. These miserable men agreed to take up arms, all in one day, murder their oppressors, and seize upon the government. But their impatience for liberty, disconcerted their plot. Some of the conspirators stabbed their masters, and set fire to their houses, before the appointed time; but finding themselves unable to resist the whole force of the island, which their premature exploit had collected, they fled to the mountains, where, being continually joined by deserters from the plantations, they incessantly made destructive inroads. At length the whole military body marched against them. They beat them in several skirmishes; many were slain and taken prisoners; and the rest dispersed into the woods and rocks. All the prisoners were shot, hanged, or burnt. Those who were supposed to be the chief, were tied alive to gibbets, and there left to perish slowly, exposed to the scorching sun of the torrid zone. One of the chiefs was condemned to be burnt alive. He was placed sitting on the ground, his body chained to a post, when the fire was placed at his feet. He did not utter a sigh, and saw his legs burnt to cinders, with a calm firmness; but the chain that confined one of his hands being loosened, he seized one of the firebrands that consumed him, and threw it in the face of his executioner.

Two others were condemned to be hung up in iron cages, and there starved to death, in the public square of Kingston. They requested to have a good meal first, which was granted. From that day until the one on which they expired, they never complained, except of the cold during the night; but in the day time, they conversed gaily with their countrymen assembled round. On the seventh day, it was rumoured, that one of them wished to communicate an important secret to his master; 'My near relation," says Bryan Edwards, "being absent, the commanding officer sent me to hear it. I endeavoured to extract the promised information, but we could not hear his reply. I recollect that he and his companion in misery laughed immoderately at something that happened. On the following morning one of them expired without uttering a word, and the other died the next day, the ninth of his punishment." Their oppressors enjoyed the torments of these miserable wretches, whose only crime was an attempt to recover by revenge, those rights of which avarice and inhumanity had deprived them.

The culture of the Sugar Cane was not known in Jamaica till the year 1668. It was brought thither by some inhabitants of Barbadoes. One of them, Sir Thomas Moddiford, who had acquired a vast estate in Barbadoes, left that island, and settled in Jamaica. His capital, together with his skill and activity, enabled him to clear an immense tract of land. Others led by his example, and the hope of gain, pursued the same course ; and money being plenty, by reason of the rich prizes which the pirates were constantly bringing in, they purchased slaves, and other necessaries for the rising plantations.

The hoe, or the spade, were necessarily used when the islands were first cleared of wood ; as the plough could not go among the roots of the trees. Before the forests were removed, slavery was unhappily introduced; and, as usual, effectually prevented all farther improvement. The Negroes have ever since been obliged to scratch the ground with the hoe; so that the agriculture of the islands remains in the same rude state in which it was 150 years ago.

In the West Indies, the slave system seems to have totally arrested the progress of rural improvement. The discomfort and destruction of the labourers, have ever been, and from the nature of the case, ever will be the consequences of compelling human beings to do the work of labouring cattle, in such a climate. The Creator himself has. put a broad negative on this whole system. His intention is plainly declared by the adaptation of animals and plants to the different climates which they inhabit... In no part of his works, is his beneficial economy more admirable, than in providing the inhabitants of hot regions with food, and clothing, and shelter, at a comparatively trifling expense of labour. Had the severe and incessant toil been necessary, as in cool and temperate climates, the torrid zone could never have been inhabited. This has been too decisively proved, by the fatal effects of continued hard labour on the native tribes, as well as on the more robust Negro race, in the West Indies. Into Jamaica, since its conquest by the British, have been imported not less than 850,000 Africans: and if we add to this number 40,000 previously. brought by the Spaniards, we have a total of 890,000 exclusive of all the births which have taken place since that period. And yet at this time, from the oppressive hardships under which they have laboured, the slave population is no more than 336,000! If we consider the numbers of lives that were sacrificed in procuring those slaves in Africa, and those lost by disease and the various calamities attending their voyage to the West Indies, what a tremendous aggregate of murder does the whole form! what an awful account to be laid at the doors of the slave-holders of Jamaica, and all those who have promoted the traffic! If we pursue this idea further—if we reckon the million of natives cruelly destroyed in St. Domingo—the millions who were murdered in the settlement of the other islands—in the conquest of Mexico—Peru—Brazil, and wherever the Europeans formed colonies —the mind is overwhelmed with horror.

If the humane Columbus could have had a view of the many millions of lives of the unoffending natives, that would be sacrificed in consequence of the discovery of America,— how would his soul have shrunk from the prospect! How would he have lamented that he was the discoverer of the new world!

It was found that the period of efficient productive hard labour, fulfilled by slaves after they were bought, did not exceed seven years, and that it could not refund the capital sunk on them and the property which they actuate. It was no wonder then, that the habitual purchasers of slaves, though making what they thought saving crops, got into debt. For nearly seventy years ending in 1768, the new Negroes annually imported for the use of Jamaica, cost one fourth of the value of the exports of that island to Great Britain—and the executions for debt in twenty years, ending 1791, were 80,081, amounting to £1,128,239 annually, being above one half of the value of the whole exports of the island.

Indented white servants were formerly not much better treated in the colonies than the negro slaves. Long says, that on their arrival in Jamaica, they used to be ranged in a line, like new Negroes, for the planters to pick and choose. A person who made a voyage to Jamaica in Governor Trelawney's time, says, "As we had a great many servants on board, and some of them fine tradesmen, we had soon a number of the planters who came to purchase indentures. It was affecting to see the shoal of buyers, and how the poor fellows were made to pass in review before their future tyrants, who looked at them and examined them, as if they had been so many horses. It is horrid to relate the barbarities that some poor starved creatures who came by another ship, complained of; a word, or a wrong look was construed a design to mutiny; and hunger, handcuffs, and a cat-o'-nine tails, was immediately the punishment. I could not help a crowd of thoughts, which pressed too fast upon me; sometimes, with sighs, I remembered the happy climate, and the dear acquaintance I had left behind. Britannia rose to my view, all gay, with native freedom blest, the seat of arts, the nurse of learning, and the friend of every virtue; where the meanest swain, with quiet ease, possesses the fruits of his hard toil, without disturbance; while I was now to settle in a place not half inhabited, cursed with intestine broils, where slavery was established, and the poor toiling wretches worked in the sultry heat, and never knew the sweets of liberty, or reaped the advantage of their painful industry, in a place, which except the verdure of its fields, had nothing to recommend it.'

The following description of the punishments of slaves, is taken from Sir Hans Sloane, who appears to have been an advocate for slavery, and attempts to defend what he thus describes:— "The punishments for crimes of slaves are usually, for rebellions, burning them, by nailing them down on the ground with crooked sticks on every limb, and then applying the fire by degrees from the feet and hands, burning them gradually up to the head, whereby their pains are extravagant. (Rebellion is thus defined by an act of Assembly: *'Every slave that shall run away, and continue but for the space of twelve months, shall be deemed rebellious'*). For crimes of a lesser nature, chopping off half of the foot with an axe. For running away, they put iron ring's of great weight on their ancles, or pottocks about their necks, which are iron rings with two long necks riveted to them, or a spur in the mouth. For negligence, they are usually whipped by the overseers with lance wood switches, till they be bloody,—being first tied up by the hands.—

After they are whipped till they are raw, some put on their skins pepper and salt, to make them smart ; at other times, their masters will drop melted wax on their skins, and use several very exquisite torments."

In a history of Jamaica, published in the year 1740, the author thus describes the situation of the slaves: "I incline to touch the hardships which these poor creatures suffer, in the tenderest manner, from a particular regard which I owe to many of their masters; but I can't conceal their sad circumstances entirely. The most trivial error is punished with a terrible whipping. I have seen their bodies all in a gore of blood, the skin tore off their backs with the cruel whip, beaten pepper and salt rubbed in the wounds, and a large stick of sealing wax dropped leisurely upon them. It is no wonder if the horrid pain of such inhuman tortures incline them to rebel; at the same time, it must be confessed, they are generally very perverse, which is owing to the many disadvantages they lie under, and the bad example they daily see. Their owners set aside for each a small parcel of ground, and allow them the Sundays to manure it. "Tis surprising to see the mean shifts to which these poor creatures are reduced. You'll see them daily about twelve o'clock, when they turn in from work, till two, scraping the dunghills at every gentleman's door for bones, which if they are so happy as to find, they break extremely small, boil them, and eat the broth. When these slaves first arrive, 'tis observed, they are simple and very innocent creatures; but they soon turn to be roguish enough: and when they come to be whipt, urge the example of the whites, for an excuse of their faults. They believe every Negro goes to their native country after death: this thought is so agreeable, that it cheers the poor creatures, and makes the burden of life easy, which otherwise would be quite intolerable. They look on death as a blessing. 'Tis indeed surprising to see with what courage and intrepidity some of them will meet their fate, and be merry in their last moments. They are quite transported to think their slavery is at an end, and that they shall revisit their happy native shores, and see their old friends and acquaintances. When a Negro is about to expire, his fellow-slaves kiss him, wish him a good journey, and send their hearty recommendations to their relations in Guinea. They make no lamentations, but with a great deal of joy inter his body, firmly believing he is gone home and happy.

"They have here the severest ways of

punishing slaves. Some that twice strike a white man, they starve to death, with a loaf hanging before their mouths: I have seen these unfortunate wretches gnaw the flesh off their shoulders, and expire in all the frightful agonies of one under the most horrid tortures. Perhaps, indeed, such severities may in some sort be excused, when we consider the state of the country, and how impossible it would be to live amidst such numbers of slaves, without watching their conduct with the greatest strictness, and punishing their faults with the utmost severity."

By the early, iniquitous laws of this island: "If any slave strikes any person, he shall for the first offence be severely whipped—for the second, be severely whipped, his nose slit, and face burnt—for the third offence, death, or any other punishment that two justices and three freeholders may think fit.

"Any person may ruinate and destroy any plantation deserted for the space of two months, lest it become a receptacle for fugitives.

"Every officer shall, upon notice given him of the haunt of any runaway Negroes, raise a party of men, and pursue and take the said runaways, alive or dead.—If any slave, by punishment from his owner, suffer in life or limb, none shall be liable to the law for the same ;—but whoever shall kill a slave out of wilfulness, wantonness, or bloody-mindedness, shall suffer three months imprisonment, and pay £50 to the owner of the slave.

"If any person kill a slave stealing, or running away, or found by night out of his owner's ground, road or common path, such person shall not be subject to any damage or action for the same.

"All owners of *Slaves, horses, or any sorts of cattle, &c.* shall give a just and true account of all *Slaves, horses, or other cattle, &c.* as are belonging to them.

"Those that go out in the parties to reduce the Negroes, shall receive for every rebellious Negro that shall be killed, bringing in the head to any justice, £40."

A slave-ship from Africa struck on some shoals called the *Morant Keys*, near Jamaica, in the night. The officers and seamen landed in their boats, leaving the slaves on board, in their irons and shackles. When morning came, it was discovered, that the Negroes had got out of their irons, and were busy in making rafts, upon which they placed the women and children, the men attending on them, whilst they drifted before the wind towards the island, where the seamen had landed. If the minds of the English had not been hardened by the slave-trade, against every feeling of humanity, they must have been moved by so interesting a scene; they would have been eager to repair their former cruel neglect, and to lend them, though late, their best assistance. But, from an apprehension that the Negroes would consume the water and provisions which they had landed, although they were so near Jamaica that they could have easily procured assistance in a few hours, they came to a resolution to destroy them; and as the poor wretches approached the shore, they fired upon them, and destroyed between three and four hundred! Out of the whole cargo, only thirty-three or four were saved; they were brought to Kingston, where they were sold by public auction.

Henry Coor, who had resided fifteen years in Jamaica, as a mill-wright, and some part of the time had been a proprietor of slaves himself, related the following circumstances: Once, when dining with an overseer, an old woman, who had run away a few days, was brought home with her hands tied behind her. After dinner, the overseer, with a clerk named Bakewell, took the woman to the hot-house, a place for the sick, and where the stocks are in one of the rooms. H. Coor went to work in the mill, about a hundred yards off, and hearing a most distressful cry from that house, he asked his men who, and what it was? They said, they thought it was old Quasheba. About five o'clock the noise ceased, and about the time he was leaving work, Bakewell came to him, apparently in great spirits, and said to him, 'Well, Mr. Coor, old Quasheba is dead. We took her to the stocks' room; the overseer threw a rope over the beam; I was Jack Ketch, and hauled her up, till her feet were off the ground. The overseer locked the door, and took the key with him, until I now returned with a slave into the stocks, and found her dead." H. Coor said, "You have killed her; I heard her cry all the afternoon." He answered with an oath, "She was good for nothing, what signifies killing such an old woman as her." H. Coor said, "Bakewell, you shock me!" and left him. The next morning his men told him, they had helped to bury her; so here it rested, till another affair brought it on the carpet. The poultry keeper, a girl about eleven or twelve years of age, brought the overseer a young duck that had died, to clear herself of having killed it; but that not satisfying him, he beat her very severely, and then forced her to eat up the duck, intestines, feathers, and all, threatening her with five times as much beating if she did not. The girl thinking more would kill her, tore and eat every bit of it. In the evening she complained to her mother, who went and complained to the attorney who managed the estate, which belonged to Mr. Beckford, of that and other cruelties of the overseer; and amongst the rest, told him the story of old Quasheba, referring for proof to Mr. Coor, who was on the estate. The attorney appeared very angry at the time, sent for Mr. Coor, and asked him how he could see his employer s slaves murdered without informing him of it. Mr. Coor told him, that such cruelties were so common on the estate, that fie had thought. no more of it. The overseer suffered no legal punishment, and went on as usual.

H. Coor said he did not think severity necessary: he had proved it himself. A gang of slaves fell under his care, which had previously been under the management of one George White. White had kept a sharp discipline over them; he generally flogged them very severely for the smallest faults, so that he reduced them both in their persons and faculties. They were never without sores, from his cruelty. The flogging disabled them from using the little leisure they had in working their grounds, which was their chief support. Hence they suffered from want, and were subject to theft. When these slaves came under Mr. Coor's care, he used them kindly, and promised rewards for good behaviour. In a few months' time, from a poor, shabby, ill-looking, dispirited gang, they became fat, sleek, lively, and worked as cheerfully as ever he saw workmen in England. Good treatment changed their very morals; he could have trusted them with anything. Mr. Coor being a lieutenant, was once ordered out after outlaws; the colonel gave him leave to arm his own slaves for sergeant's guard of the white militia. They pitched their huts round his, saying, they would all die, sooner than he should be hurt; and they served with fidelity. These slaves were under his care thirteen years and a half, during which he never flogged one of them; they would have been more ashamed of a small tap from him, than of a hundred lashes from their former master. 'They were grateful in the highest degree: on Sunday they would often bring him a fowl as a present; and they never killed a hog, but they saved some choice part for him: he could mention many other instances of their gratitude and affection for him.

On Shrewsbury estate, the overseer sent for a slave, and in talking with him, he hastily struck him on the head with a small hanger, and gave him two stabs about the waist. The slave said, "Overseer, you have killed me." He pushed him out of the piazza; the slave went home, and died that night; he was buried and no more said about it. This man was called a very valuable overseer, as he worked the slaves hard, and made great crops of sugar.

At Mr. Coor's first going to the island, a common flogging would put him in a tremble, so that he did not feel right for the rest of the day; but by degrees it became so habitual, that he thought no more of seeing a black man's head cut off, than he should of a butcher cutting off the head of a calf. Hercules Ross, who resided twenty-one years in Jamaica, gave the following information: hearing the cries of some poor wretch from an inclosure, he looked through, and saw a young female suspended by the wrists to a tree, swinging to and fro; her toes could barely touch the ground, »: and her body was exceedingly agitated. There was no whipping, and the master was just by, seemingly motionless, so that he could not immediately account for the appearance of extreme torture; but on looking more attentively, he saw in the master's hand a stick of fire, which he held so as to touch her as she swung. He continued this torture with unmoved countenance, until H. Ross called on him to desist, and throwing stones at him over the fence, stopped it. This man was brought to no punishment, This gentleman said, that there were in Kingston many people who bought on speculation those slaves which were left after the first day's sale of a cargo of these wretched people. He had often seen the refuse landed, and sent to be sold, in a very wretched state; sometimes in the agonies of death ; he had known them to expire in the piazza of the auctioneer. They were sometimes sold as low as a dollar.

Dr. Pinkhard informs us, that in walking through Kingston, he observed sixteen or eighteen Negroes linked in a sort of harness, and forming a regular team, drawing an immense trunk of mahogany, conducted by a driver with a cartwhip, who went whistling at their side, and flogging them on, precisely as an English carter does his horses. Similar well-authenticated instances of cruelty and oppression, might be produced to almost any extent; but it is needless, as it is admitted on all hands, that *formerly* great cruelties were practised in the slave colonies. 'Thirty or forty years ago, when the subject was first brought before public notice, the colonists denied the existence of such things, and described slavery as a state of great comfort and happiness, in the same manner as the advocates of the system do at the present day. The truth of those accounts has however, been established beyond all doubt, and is abundantly proved by the late writers and speakers in defence of slavery. Alexander Barclay, who resided twenty-one years in Jamaica, and published a defence of slavery in 1827, in which he describes the present state of the slaves, as one of great enjoyment, informs us, "that at no very distant period, the master's power of punishing his slaves, was little restrained by law; and was exercised to a great extent, by the subordinate white people and the drivers."

"Ten years ago, chains were in common use on the plantations, for punishing criminal slaves." This writer acknowledges in many other particulars, the existence in former times, of those evils of slavery, which the advocates of the system utterly denied, at the time referred to, in as strong terms as he himself, and other modern defenders of slavery deny the evils charged upon the system at the present time.

The *truth* is, however, continually coming out—it is not so difficult to ascertain as it was formerly. The public documents of the West Indians themselves, are a sufficient proof of all that the abolitionists assert. Almost any West Indian newspaper will prove it.

[PECKHAM.]

London: — S. Bagster, Jun., Printer, 14, Bartholomew Close.

SELECTED FROM VARIOUS AUTHORS

Would you like to buy a copy of
' A HISTORY OF JAMAICA '
by William James Gardner ?

Order Online!

PLEASE VISIT:
http://www.diamondbooks.ca

HUGE SAVINGS ON BULK ORDERS
(10 copies, 20 copies, 50 copies, 100 copies, 500 copies, 1000 copies)

Please send your request at:
http://www.diamondbooks.ca/bulkorder

A HISTORY

of

JAMAICA

FROM ITS DISCOVERY BY
THE CHRISTOPHER COLUMBUS TO THE PRESENT TIME

OUT OF MANY, ONE PEOPLE

WILLIAM JAMES GARDNER

Original Edition

ISBN : 978-1773750774

HISTORIC JAMAICA

A PICTURESQUE TOUR OF THE ISLAND OF JAMAICA (1875).
KINGSTON, & PORT ROYAL. FROM WINDSOR FARM.

SPECIAL EDITION

ILLUSTRATED

FRANK CUNDALL

Original Edition

ISBN : 978-1988942889

FOR PRINTS, PLEASE VIT:
http://www.diamondbooks.ca

STUDIES

IN

JAMAICA HISTORY

PROVIDING PARTICULARS
OF A FEW OF THE EPOCHS IN ITS
HISTORY
FOR TOURISTS AND OTHERS

FRANK CUNDALL

Original Edition
ISBN : 978-1988942889

FOR PRINTS, PLEASE VIT:
http://www.diamondbooks.ca

NOTES

NOTES

NOTES

NOTES